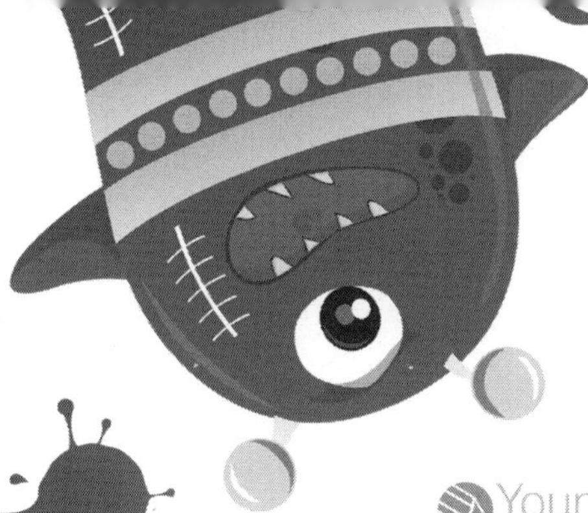

YoungWriters®
Est. 1991

MONSTER POETRY

Beastly Creations

Edited By Debbie Killingworth

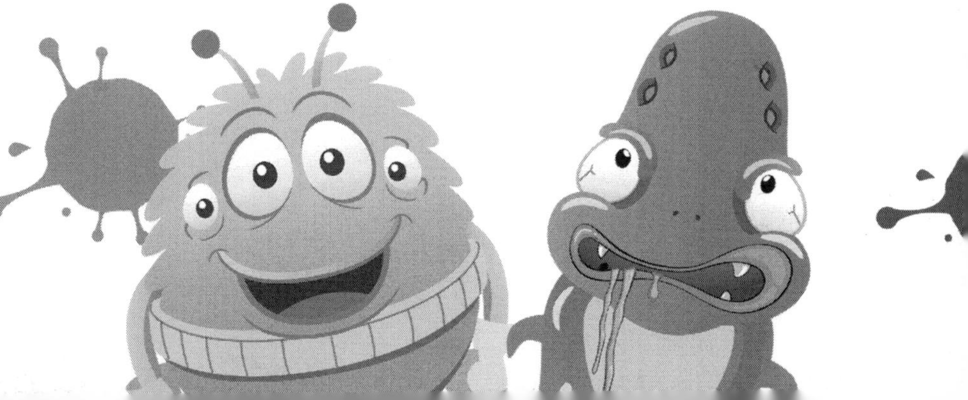

First published in Great Britain in 2023 by:

Young Writers
Remus House
Coltsfoot Drive
Peterborough
PE2 9BF
Telephone: 01733 890066
Website: www.youngwriters.co.uk

All Rights Reserved
Book Design by Ashley Janson
© Copyright Contributors 2023
Softback ISBN 978-1-80459-757-6

Printed and bound in the UK by BookPrintingUK
Website: www.bookprintinguk.com
YB0556G

Foreword

Young Writers was created in 1991 with the express purpose of promoting and encouraging creative writing. Each competition we create is tailored to the relevant age group, giving each child the inspiration and incentive to create their own piece of writing, whether it's a poem or a short story. We truly believe that seeing it in print gives pupils a sense of achievement and pride in their work and themselves.

Our latest competition, Monster Poetry, focuses on uncovering the different techniques used in poetry and encouraging pupils to explore new ways to write a poem. Using a mix of imagination, expression and poetic styles, this anthology is an impressive snapshot of the inventive, original and skilful writing of young people today. These poems showcase the creativity and talent of these budding new writers as they learn the skills of writing, and we hope you are as entertained by them as we are.

Contents

Canon Barnett Primary School, London

Aliza Ahmed (8)	1
Maryam Imam (7)	2
Aiza Miah (8)	4
Zaynab Islam Chowdhury (8)	5
Zarah Oloyade (7)	6

Clifton Green Primary School, Clifton

Lola Read-Rennie (8)	7
Isabelle Duffy (8)	8
Oscar Woloszyk (8)	10
Kadisha Elijah (10)	11
Rill Anderson (10)	12
Layla Scrivener (7)	13
Jakob Williams (7)	14
Faith Falcone (9)	15
Finley Pay (8)	16
Albie Thompson (7)	17
Katy Brown (8)	18
Grace Welch-Fisher (8)	19
Joshitha Senthil Kumar (10)	20
Oscar Rynkiewicz (7)	21
Rachael Ogunnowo (7)	22
Rebeccah Ogunnowo (7)	23
Daisy Read-Rennie (6)	24
Kitty Chapman (8)	25
Katie Sznaze (9)	26
Frankie Littlewood (7)	27
Matilda Riddle (7)	28
Jake Chapman (6)	29

Crofton Anne Dale Junior School, Stubbington

Olivia Bygrave (9)	30
Freya Carstens (10)	32
Isabelle Kerrigan (9)	33
Erin Wood (10)	34
Orlagh Smith (9)	36
Marlie Vincent (8)	37
Alexia Cirmis (10)	38
Flo Ashton (10)	40
Evelyn Taylor (9)	42
Shan Xin Cheung (9)	43
Claudia Elkington (9)	44
Ruby Phillips (10)	46
Eva Mountford (10)	47
Jessica-Lily Hale (9)	48
Faye Ali (10)	49
Sophia Lee (9)	50
Louie Charlesworth (10)	51
Malakai Eriemo (9)	52
Oscar Keen (9)	53
Isla Allmark (9)	54
Skye Causer (10)	55
Mia Hogg (9)	56
Pari Mistry (10)	57
Olivia Ward-Saunders (10)	58
Eleanor Try (10)	59
Henry Gelder (10)	60
Fraya Pugh (10)	61
Ella Griffiths (10)	62
Isabella Withers (10)	63
Kaleesi Joy (9)	64
Isla G (10)	65
Elliot Deutekom (9)	66
Aidan Royal (10)	67

Lily Hatherley (8)	68
Alexa Wu (10)	69
Sophie Amey (9)	70
Imogen Stanning (10)	71
Poppy Hewitt (10)	72
Lydia Bradford (10)	73
Jackson Blease (9)	74
Finch Grant Ros (8)	75
Jonathan Higgins (10)	76
Solomon Phillips (9)	77
Adelaide Davies Vaughan (10)	78
Sophie Cogdell (10)	79
Henry Crocker (9)	80
Thomas White (9)	81
Jazzy Hudson (10)	82
Amelie Williams (9)	83
Leo Kington (9)	84
Lukas Davies (9)	85
Eva Register (10)	86
Henry Graham (9)	87
Katie Nicholls (10)	88
Woody Rawson (9)	89
Alfie Ludlow-Fisher (10)	90
Ruby Wallace (9)	91
Isla Knott (9)	92
Pippa Clarke (9)	93
Demi Ward (9)	94
Elliot Vaughan (9)	95
Charlie Warburton (10)	96
Joshua Knight (9)	97
Ruben Cresswell (9)	98
Andrew Baillie (9)	99
Jaspar Ball (10)	100
Lucas Day (9)	101
Caelan Fielding (9)	102

Great Bardfield Primary School, Great Bardfield

Mila Kiddy (9)	103
Ivy-Lilly Humphreys (7)	104

Holy Trinity CE Primary School, Cheltenham

James Russett (10)	105
Cressida Bird (11)	106
Mona El Aambri	107
Freddie Hinton (11)	108
Teddy Longworth (10)	109
Atticus Harbinson (11)	110
Anthony Hawkins (10)	111
Olivia Upton (11)	112
Clemence Sandeman (11)	113
Daniel Leong (11)	114
Betty Brazil (11)	115
Aurelie Whitelow (11)	116
Cordelia Griffin (11)	117
Richard Killworth (10)	118
Skye Franks-Bayntun (11)	119
Sophie Nayna (11)	120
Isaac Jones (9)	121
Zoia Kobzarenko (10)	122
Milan Bencsik (10)	123
Esther Chindudzi (8)	124
Ann Sajan (11)	125
Amit Rajesh (11)	126
Milly Pargeter (9)	127
Eric Ameri (8)	128
Ewan Somerville (8)	129
Lucy Griffiths (9)	130
Aleks Skrzynski (11)	131
Laura Shone (9)	132
Rex Musasa (9)	133
Amelie Beckett (8)	134
Torin Whitelow (9)	135
Ben Gregory (8)	136
Diana Stavreva (9)	137
Lottie Greenwood (9)	138
Ilias El Aambri (8)	139
Amelie Weeden (9)	140
Leo Turley (9)	141
Henry Pardoe (8)	142
Henry Hatcher (9)	143
Ralegh Steel (9)	144

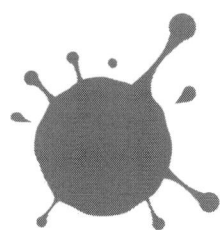

The Poems

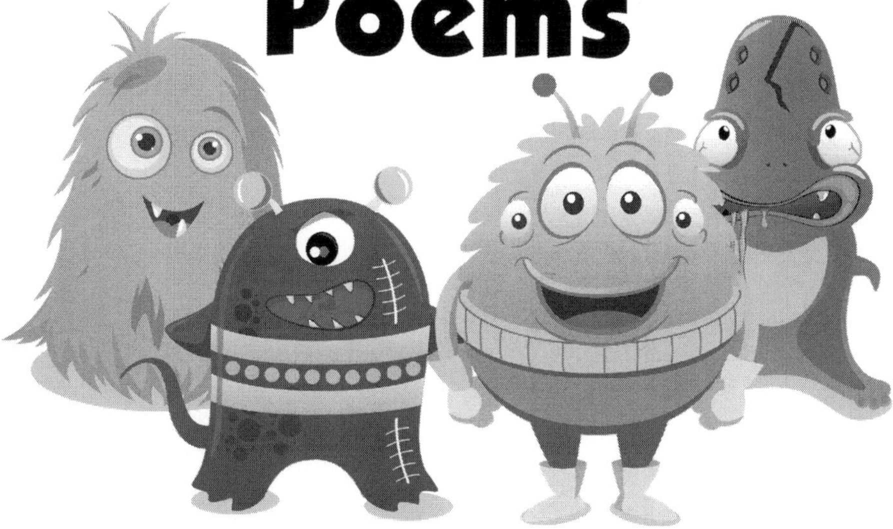

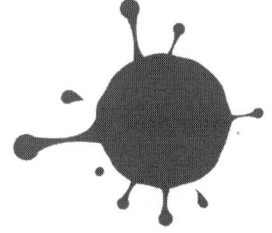

My Blue Monster

Monster, monster, where are you?
Monster, monster, I need you
The sky has fallen down
What can you do?

I can fly you to the moon
Or take you to the zoo
But do not be so blue
Or the flowers will not bloom
And the day will not gloom

The monster stomps
If you want to be a blue monster
Well now's your chance
Because everyone's doing the monster dance
You jump stomp your feet
Wave your arms around
Stretch them up and down
Then touch the ground
Because we're doing the monster dance.

Aliza Ahmed (8)
Canon Barnett Primary School, London

The Monster

The monster is a shape-shifter
He can change into any mister
But his favourite self
Has legs like boiled eggs
And toes like pegs
The monster is hairy
And it looks quite scary
But don't be afraid, don't be wary
The monster has branches for arms
And pancakes for palms
His head is like a giant bubble
With tentacles that flash a bright light
His eyes are the size of tennis balls
His pupils are white
The monster crashed and landed on Earth
Mighty in girth
The monster crashed and made a big mess
But soon felt distressed
He looked around and saw kids playing with paper crowns

But when they saw the monster, it gave them a big frown
To show he wasn't just a monster
He played with them all day
And learned that kindness goes a long way
And though he came from outer space
He found a home in a new place.

Maryam Imam (7)
Canon Barnett Primary School, London

Scaily The Dragon

Scaily the dragon's goal is to learn and grow
Scaily the dragon loves going to school
Even when she's got a fever that turns her even more blue
She likes to study and play in the pool
She loves her numbers as they jump up and down
Like the musical notes playing in a rhyme
She loves to juggle a ball to its net
And wiggle her tail on a hula hoop
Her best time of the day is when she flames all her food away
Scaily the dragon is very kind and helpful
When you need a friend she's always there for you!

Aiza Miah (8)
Canon Barnett Primary School, London

Monica's First Day Out!

Monica was allowed to have fun
She could play in the sea with the sun
She passed her aunt that makes magic potions
She swam very deep
Until it was almost time to go to sleep
She found a scary cave
Was there anything inside that she could save?
Seashells or maybe human things
Like necklaces or maybe earrings
Sadly it was time for her to go
Because she knew her parents would say no!

Zaynab Islam Chowdhury (8)
Canon Barnett Primary School, London

The Kind Monster

Luna the monster is loving, caring, helpful and always kind to people
He would go to a cave and give people food and water
My monster's friends are humans
He is nice to everyone and people are also nice to him
He loves eating worms which he enjoys a lot
Luna the monster is fluffy like the clouds
My monster is small, cute, stripy and loved.

Zarah Oloyade (7)
Canon Barnett Primary School, London

Pete The Monster

Under my bed lives a monster called Pete.
Sometimes I get scared that he will grab my feet.
He is hairy and scary and his fur is red.
I hide under my covers on top of my bed.
One night I heard him let out a growl,
I think he trumped, the smell was foul.
I decided to be brave and have a closer peep,
That is when I found out Pete was really quite sweet.
He is red and furry and has a big toothy grin.
He has purple spots on his tummy and a big beard on his chin.
I'm not scared anymore because I realised Pete is kind
And all it took was me to be brave one time.

Lola Read-Rennie (8)
Clifton Green Primary School, Clifton

The Monster Under Your Bed

Have you ever thought about what lurks under your bed?
Did you imagine it or was it all in your head?
The bedroom is dark and the clock is midnight,
But what was that noise? Was it a mouse?
It definitely came from inside the house
So you take a breath and bravely threw back the cover.
You lean over the bed and take a peek,
One eye is staring back, looking bleak.
He opens his mouth and hanging down are two very sharp fangs.
You jump back up and try your best to hide
But a scuffle is heard, might be the monster or maybe a bird.
Long arms start to creep towards you, getting closer
So from the bedside table, you grab your bedtime drink and splash the thing.

Straight away the monster starts to shrink,
A blue puddle is all that's left behind
And a memory is all you will find.

Isabelle Duffy (8)
Clifton Green Primary School, Clifton

Dragon Demon

As big as a 33 floor skyscraper,
This dragon is not to be met with.
128 feet tall, its giant body can absorb anything.
About 10,000 years ago it destroyed every village in its path,
It ruined every city and left it all in ruins.

Everything they pull at him is destroyed in seconds.
With his sharp claws,
He can instantly break through any type of metal.
Diving underwater is no problem for this beast.

With no friends, he is thirsty for blood.
Where did be come from? Nobody knows.
One thing everybody knows he is bad!

Oscar Woloszyk (8)
Clifton Green Primary School, Clifton

Death

Death is a monster.
Death cannot be cured.
The Bible says people should live one hundred and twenty but Death destroys you so you cannot live long.
Some people die when being born,
Others die when they are young.
Death is caused by many things
Like accidents and food poisoning.
Death can also come without warning.
Death cannot be cured by medicine.
Doctors might try but there is no cure.
This monster is conquered by eternal life in heaven where it has no power.
That is my greatest joy.

Kadisha Elijah (10)
Clifton Green Primary School, Clifton

Boo's Blues

Boo's blues come from friends,
Tears fall from his glasses lens,
Covered in green fur,
Maybe because he murmurs.
I don't know why, he thought,
How can he be taught?
Maybe it's because of his three eyes,
Why can't they just compromise?

Boo's happiness comes from friends,
Covered in glasses lens,
Filled with red fur,
How could this occur?
I don't know how, he thought,
With five eyes
Who could hide that disguise,
Sold!

Rill Anderson (10)
Clifton Green Primary School, Clifton

The Happy Monster

Monster, monster under my stairs,
I hear your giggles when no one is there.

I heard your name was Mr Fluff,
You think you're really mean and tough.

One day I'll be brave and check under the stairs
And prove to you I'm not scared.

When I do we'll be such good friends,
A true friendship that will never end.

I don't believe you're mean and tough,
You're just a rainbow monster covered in fluff.

Layla Scrivener (7)
Clifton Green Primary School, Clifton

Elemental Dragon

Elemento was a monster who lived in a cave,
He went to Monster School for monsters who couldn't behave.
The other monsters at the school made fun of his three heads,
They even made fun of him because he didn't have any legs.
He moved to New York and got quite a shock,
Suddenly he could make thunder's fire ice blocks
But the people in the city went nasty or cried,
They showed him New York's three-headed monster school.

Jakob Williams (7)
Clifton Green Primary School, Clifton

Monster Poetry - Beastly Creations

Don't Be Afraid Of Me!

I go by the name of Bloboton,
My friends call me Blob for short.
i am funny, nice and a little bit spooky
And my favourite hobby is sport.
People scream when they see me,
But I always wonder why.
"Don't be afraid of me," I say,
"I wouldn't hurt a fly.
Don't be afraid of me,
Not all monsters are the same.
I'm a big green friendly monster
And Bloboton is my name."

Faith Falcone (9)
Clifton Green Primary School, Clifton

Why Monsters Deserve Better!

Why do we treat monsters so foully?
They have feelings just like us.
We should treat them very proudly,
Treat them how they treat us.
As if, take my monster called Jelly,
She can be rather silly.
Also Jelly supports not just me but everybody.
Maybe one day she'll find somebody who understands her.
They deserve better because they really try to help us!
They don't try to disgust us!

Finley Pay (8)
Clifton Green Primary School, Clifton

Footy Monster

Footy Monster came from space
And found a new place.
He is very mischievous and made lots of mates,
At the football ground, he was naughty
And played tricks by shape-shifting.
Footy Monster was very hairy,
But definitely not scary!
He has three eyes but never cries.
There is just one thing that nobody knew,
His fangs grew and grew.

Albie Thompson (7)
Clifton Green Primary School, Clifton

Family's Broken Heart

A scary wolf with very sharp teeth,
But very gentle and fluffy with big brown eyes.
Always full of crazy games and always playful.
Sadly gone but never forgotten.
We will always love and remember you in our hearts forever.
Some people thought you were scary but you were very sweet like cotton candy.
In my heart you were always my best friend.

Katy Brown (8)
Clifton Green Primary School, Clifton

The Cute Mermaid Monster

In the deep warm ocean
Stands a tall castle.
A mermaid makes a potion,
She loves to dance
And wants to do it in the world above.
She wants to find romance.
Will she find love?
Maybe with a prince in France!
Will her potion turn her human
So she can be seen as a cute girl
Instead of the monster people think she is.

Grace Welch-Fisher (8)
Clifton Green Primary School, Clifton

Sakuras - The Blossom Serpent

S he grows each shiny sequin scale
A nd her Sakura story will prevail
K eeping her beauties in her ghostly trail
U nder her eye, no flower can fail
R avenous for a feast, she gorges on more
A nd she rules over all Sakuras, that's the law
S ee here, she loves Sakuras, oh Sakuras galore.

Joshitha Senthil Kumar (10)
Clifton Green Primary School, Clifton

Cookie

There was a monster named Cookie.
He was not even a bit spooky.
He had five eyes
He liked to eat ice.
He had spikes that were purple.
He walked as slow as a turtle.
He teleported from one place to another.
He also had a sister and a brother.
He liked to swim and play games.
He could breathe fire with flames.

Oscar Rynkiewicz (7)
Clifton Green Primary School, Clifton

Dragon In The Sky

The tip of a spike,
The point of a claw,
The flash of a flame,
That's all I saw.

Ran off and hid,
That's all I did
Until all the sky cleared
And the signs disappeared.
The dragon was far and high,
I wish I had waved goodbye.

Rachael Ogunnowo (7)
Clifton Green Primary School, Clifton

Dragon Fire

Kissing a dragon is dangerous
Even if you love one a lot
It's hard to give one a cuddle
His breath is much too hot.

The dragon's breath is fire
The noble, the valiant
May quench the dragon's fire
To free the world from fear.

Rebeccah Ogunnowo (7)
Clifton Green Primary School, Clifton

I Am A Monster

There is a monster in my house.
It is not quiet like a mouse.
She shouts a lot and makes a mess.
She likes to wear a pretty dress.
She loves to eat sweetcorn for her tea.
If you have not already guessed the monster is me.

Daisy Read-Rennie (6)
Clifton Green Primary School, Clifton

Clifton Greeny

This is Clifton Greeny,
He is really weeny,
He lives in Clifton Woods
And likes to wear tops with hoods.

This is Clifton Greeny,
He really is a meany,
He has big wings
And he likes park swings.

Kitty Chapman (8)
Clifton Green Primary School, Clifton

Oh Monster, Monster!

When I'm sad, you're with me.
When I'm happy, you cheer with me.
When I cry, you cry too.
When I laugh, you laugh too.
When I play, you join in.
When you're away,
I feel alone.

Katie Sznaze (9)
Clifton Green Primary School, Clifton

Boggy

B ig eyes so he can see his friends
O ne big mouth
G reen feet
G iant green hands
Y ou should be his friend because he is nice and he is friendly to people.

Frankie Littlewood (7)
Clifton Green Primary School, Clifton

Maggie The Monster

Maggie the monster had a wish
That one day she would be a fish.
She met the queen who was very mean
And put her in a dish.

Matilda Riddle (7)
Clifton Green Primary School, Clifton

Gooey In The Park

Gooey is sad
But he is quite bad.
But then he flew off with his wings
And as he does he always sings.

Jake Chapman (6)
Clifton Green Primary School, Clifton

A Monstrous Rescue

Sable the monster, furry, short and green.
She is very rarely mean.

One day, when out for a swim
Her best friend Willow also dived in.

Sable the shapeshifter who was then a fish
Hadn't noticed something was amiss.

Sable heard Willow shouting for help
She saw that Willow was wrapped in the kelp!

Sable knew what she had to do.
She whirled around quickly to turn into something new.

Shimmering cyan tail, magical magenta hair.
Courageous and strong, a mermaid who was fair.

Sable raced towards Willow as fast as she was able
But when she reached her, it was tougher than cable!

Monster Poetry - Beastly Creations

Sable turned into a swordfish as elegant as can be.
She cut through the kelp as easy as 1, 2... she was free!

Sable raced towards the surface as fast as a cheetah!
No one and nothing could ever beat her!

The water was warmer the higher they got,
But Sable knew something to make it real hot!

Twisting and turning she broke through the waves
Sable turned into a dragon ever so brave.

She flapped her great wings, as dark as night,
Her way home was quite a long flight.

Before my poem comes to an end
Just remember that monsters can save their friends.

Olivia Bygrave (9)
Crofton Anne Dale Junior School, Stubbington

The Monster Under The Desk

When I go to school under my desk
I have a little monster called Ben.
Lots of people think Ben is an ogre
And the devil with fifty spots.
Ben is my friend, he helps me,
We have an age difference, though he's five, I'm ten.
Sometimes Ben's inner child comes to play
And messes the class with crimes.
Although everyone is scared of Ben
We're best friends so we just go with the flow.
We both like colouring till Ben gets bored
Then he grows a monster tree
But sometimes Ben gets sloppy and mean
So he tells funny stories but they don't rhyme.
Every lunchtime Ben digs holes to hide his monster accessory
Because Ben is always naughty
So he gets told off but he gets applause.
This is the life with Ben but you don't want to meet his sis.

Freya Carstens (10)
Crofton Anne Dale Junior School, Stubbington

Serpent In The Night

In the night you can't fall asleep
Not knowing if you are in for a big threat.
As you stare into the abysmal night an alarm alerts your brain.
It is a cat, dog or sheep?
As you cower in your bed a gush of breeze breaks through, a clack on your window.
A light flickers out as you stand frozen with a lighter which is to all your delight.
As you run to your lorry you think of frozen curry.
As you scurry a sign appears on your window screen.
As you look you see beautiful patterns.
The monster has long sharp fangs.
It has rainbow scales and dragon wings with great talons.
As you realise you're trapped you begin to worry.
You get out your lorry with a big worry.
You flick on the light to scare it away.
As it scurries away you give it some curry.

Isabelle Kerrigan (9)
Crofton Anne Dale Junior School, Stubbington

Ira, The Irish Water Phoenix

High, high up in the sky you'll find the most magnificent creature of all time.
She lives in all terrains, above the clouds and below the crashing waves.
She is known as Ira, Ira the Irish water phoenix.
With her silver, green and metallic blue appearance
And crown of feathers on her head,
She is Irish royalty from top to talon.
As rare as a purple banana and the will of the sea inside,
This phoenix is one of the most beautiful beings ever to be alive.
Although a bird in appearance, Ira couldn't be less alike.
When she dives towards the sea, her wings clump to her sides,
And once she's in the water, she disappears like a snow hare in snow.

Blue eyes become waterproof, her feathers deflect the cold.
Beating her wings gracefully, a new story unfolds.

Erin Wood (10)
Crofton Anne Dale Junior School, Stubbington

Melly Melly

Melly Melly you are smelly and eat jelly
While watching telly
And you know if you are smelly you are deadly.
Sometimes you scare Ellie
But are there any other ways to scare Ellie?

Melly Melly you have one eye and have a patched eye
You have a blue bow and four pink tentacles.
You have two gold earrings for both ears
And have dark green stripes on your left ear
And purple stripes on the other.
You have yellow gloves and slit pupils.
Finally, you have a ghost body
And a split orange tongue
And your body's skin is light purple.

You live in a cave far away from here.
Your cave is so huge that it can fit ten elephants.
It has crystals that whistle.
Your cave is in a forest
But you leave when it's August.

Orlagh Smith (9)
Crofton Anne Dale Junior School, Stubbington

Scallywig

Scallywig likes to dig and her favourite animal is a pig.
She is gleeful all day but especially in the month of May.
She likes to sleep tucked up in a tree and loves to play with the bees.
When it rains, her skin will change.
She uses this to attract her prey and stores her food in her tummy all day.
When the clock strikes midnight you will be in for a fright.
The children sleep tight in their beds unaware of what's ahead.
The children scream because Scallywig looks mean.
She looks over the bed with her eyes so red and soon forgets that she has already been fed!
Her eyes then turn blue and at that moment she knew that her love for children was true.
The children were still so scared but soon realised Scallywig cared.

Marlie Vincent (8)
Crofton Anne Dale Junior School, Stubbington

Monster Joy

Splatt was a monster who loved joy and glee,
Spreading his heart out and being happy.

But some old folks thought being joyful was bad,
Making jokes about Splatt and being quite mad.

And one day they thought and one day they did
Give the monster a lesson so they went out and hid.

As quick as a blink Splatt took out his brush
The crowds all gasped as he gave it a swoosh.

All of a sudden, delighted all felt
Prancing and dancing, all reunited.

Some people questioned why they sometimes felt sad
But Splatt explained being sad was not bad.

There is no wrong emotion
It's okay to feel dread.

Don't pass it on to others
Spread kindness instead.

Alexia Cirmis (10)
Crofton Anne Dale Junior School, Stubbington

The Monster That Lives Under The Stairs

There's a monster in my house,
Under the stairs,
Sometimes you can even see him,
Giving you a glare,
With his bright orange eyes,
Like something in a nightmare.

He's brown, fluffy
And not very tall,
I think he must be clumsy
Because I heard him bump into the wall.

At night when you're asleep,
He's been really rude,
One time I found him in the kitchen,
Eating all our food.

I don't think he's really scary,
I think he pretends,
Maybe he's living in our house,
Because he'd like a friend.

So when you go to bed at night,
Be sure to take good care,
Because you might have a monster,
Living under your stairs.

Flo Ashton (10)
Crofton Anne Dale Junior School, Stubbington

Demoflower

D evilishly cute,
E xcellent at climbing,
M arvellously brave,
O utrageously bright,
F orever kind,
L ong-tailed,
O ut-of-the-box ideas,
W ise and smart,
E verlasting happiness every day,
R ed cheeks all day...

These are all things that describe Demoflower.
Demoflower lives in a tower and has the power of nature.
It's tall, it's green and it'll make you scream.
Plus it loves the taste of buttercream.
Day or night it'll give you a fright though it's actually very shy.
So please don't scream when you see this flowery thing.
He's really very shy and nice.

Evelyn Taylor (9)
Crofton Anne Dale Junior School, Stubbington

Cookie

My lovely monster is Cookie,
He loves to share his cookie.
Everyone thinks he is horrible,
But actually, he is loveable.

He's got a cool horn on his head,
He uses it to make someone dead.
He likes to use his wings to fly,
But when he goes high he will cry.

He always thinks everything is fine,
Even when someone took his things and said,
"They are mine."
He likes someone to be his buddy,
But his buddy must love studies.

His dream job is to be a scientist with his friend,
He wants to discover what happens when it is the end.
But when he asked someone to do with himself,
Everyone thought he was a strange elf.

Shan Xin Cheung (9)
Crofton Anne Dale Junior School, Stubbington

The Aliens Saved The Day

On the planet Snobble
Lives a man called Bobble
Since it always slimily rains
They have to live down the drain.

One day on the other side of Snobble
Another young man took a wobble
His name was Kain
And because of the slime rain he slipped down the drain.

When he opened his eyes
To his surprise
He saw a spaceship from a distant land
With a tall squibby man with a menacing gun in his hand.

"They're after our gold
Bobble must be told!"
As quick as a flash
To Bobble he did dash.

He screamed, "Come and save the day
With your ribble ray!"
Bobble took aim and saved the day.

Claudia Elkington (9)
Crofton Anne Dale Junior School, Stubbington

The Hairy Two

Fred is clumsy and sweet
But my goodness have you smelt his feet?
People assume he's scary but all he is is hairy.
He's scared of the dark and his middle name is Clark.
His friend, Ed wets the bed.
They're a right old pair and they easily scare.
They call themselves The Hairy Two,
Fred has a soft spot for children, it's true.
If you see him don't be scared
Because neither of you will be prepared.
He's scared of dogs but not frogs,
He loves flowers, he'll be smelling them for hours.

Now I have told you all about Fred,
Don't worry he's not under your bed,
But he may appear so listen with your ear.

Ruby Phillips (10)
Crofton Anne Dale Junior School, Stubbington

Deadly Siren

One late stormy night,
A terrifying scream coming from the distance.
Those who have explored the sea before
Don't live to tell the tale of sea folk law.
Upon the craggy rocks sat the siren
Waiting for a ship to come near,
With her flowing green seaweed hair
And her bulging red, burning eyes.
Her scaly, shimmering fish tail splashing in the waves.
Her teeth were as sharp as fangs.
She opens her mouth and cries the siren song,
Luring the ship near her.
It was so loud that the sailors had to explore and follow the sound.
Crash! The ship goes under, men screaming for help,
But it was too late, the siren had got to them.

Eva Mountford (10)
Crofton Anne Dale Junior School, Stubbington

Do You Kick Stones?

Do you kick stones whilst walking?
Do you kick stones whilst talking?
Ever wonder where the stones then go?
Well, take a seat, because I know.
Up in the mountains you will find Crunch!
Be careful though he'll eat you for lunch.
Crunch is a monster made of stones,
If you listened closely you'll hear his groans.
Each stone you kick will make him bigger,
Adding to his bulbous figure.
Every stone kicked remembers your name,
They tell Crunch to revenge their pain.
You can run, but you cannot hide,
There will always be a stone by your side.
Next time, think before kicking stones,
As Crunch will enjoy chewing your bones.

Jessica-Lily Hale (9)
Crofton Anne Dale Junior School, Stubbington

Sweetie Poem

I was born a monster
Who really liked Costa.
People are scared of me
But I just want to eat sweeties.
I can't stop it,
But now my clothes can't fit.
People think I'm scary
But really I am just really hairy.
I live with my best friend Cheery,
We are both just really merry.
I am fluffy
But when I don't get sweets I get huffy.

I love to dance and sing around
And when get given sweets I sing a beautiful sound.
Give me the best sweets and you will be amazed,
Please don't be afraid.
Even monsters can have a heart so pure
And I can eat the most sweets that's for sure.

Faye Ali (10)
Crofton Anne Dale Junior School, Stubbington

Cliff

I'm not scary, not scary at all,
You'd expect me to be big but I'm actually quite small.
My slimy tail is a sight to see
But hey, that's just me.
With my thorn-like spikes, I stand out in a crowd,
Although I am different I am very proud.
I'm mischievous, adventurous, fearless and bold,
I'm the greatest monster ever to be told.
My cheesy grin and sparkles of white
Can be seen on the darkest of nights.
With these bright orange wings that can be seen from afar,
Some might say they shine like a star.
So this is me, I am not a myth,
It's so nice to meet you,
My name is Cliff!

Sophia Lee (9)
Crofton Anne Dale Junior School, Stubbington

Monster Poetry - Beastly Creations

The Death Demon

The three-pronged horn makes it inevitable,
Through one encounter the suffering will be incredible.
The chosen one only can survive the pain,
And then the monster will be slain.

Hurry thou before it's too late,
The Death Demon awaits.
The one strike that it takes,
The enhanced blessing shan't wait.

Hurry, quick and free the souls,
From the carnage that the monster holds.
Every move the monster makes,
Holds malice in its place.

One swing - do not hesitate,
The Death Demon awaits.
Rend the Demon's inner soul,
To set us all free must be your goal.

Louie Charlesworth (10)
Crofton Anne Dale Junior School, Stubbington

Bounce From Outer Space

B is for behaviour and mine is very unpleasant.
A is for argument and Bounce gets into a lot of them when he is planning his crimes.
S is for something different will be planned every day for Bounce.
K is for king of evil basketballs.
E is for everything Bounce does is disgraceful.
T is for my twin basketball in a different galaxy.
B is for bouncing into crimes.
A is for all around the world Bounce causes crimes.
L is for learning to behave even more evil.
L is for loads of basketballs are evil but Bounce is different.

Malakai Eriemo (9)
Crofton Anne Dale Junior School, Stubbington

The Deadly Monster

Once there was a deadly monster who lived under little people's beds.
In the night he popped up in the darkness to frighten people and scare them.
His name was Bob and he was just trying to make some friends but every other monster said that he was not scary enough.
So he went under other people's beds and scared them so that he could go back to his real home and be scary like all the other monsters.
He kept moving homes to see if he would like to stay there or not.
He continued to scare but when he tried to scare someone they weren't scared so they became friends and Bob decided to live there.

Oscar Keen (9)
Crofton Anne Dale Junior School, Stubbington

Party With Monsters

Running, playing, having fun,
Monster party everyone.
Roundabouts spinning round,
Monsters like partying all night long.
After a busy day, time to pack up,
The monsters play Dinner Time.
"Winners from our play, gather round," they all say.
They all were in bed dreaming away.
They went to the marketplace
But the statue had been replaced
With a new monster's face
Who came in first place.
Peppermint stopped to tie her shoelace.
They were revealing the winner,
Peppermint who was looking at a fingerprint,
It turned out she came in first place.

Isla Allmark (9)
Crofton Anne Dale Junior School, Stubbington

I Am A Monster

I am not a man or hero
I am a villain, a monster
I am the darkness in the shadow
I am what is left in the mass after
You are no woman, you're an angel
You are a slave, you're a demon
You are the silence in the shell
You are the dusk creeping into the evening
I am a man and a hero to you
I am no villain, no monstrosity
I am the lie that devises the truth
I am the strongest viscosity
You are a woman and angel to me
You are no slave, no devil
You are whispers coming from the sea
You are the crest on the highest hill.

Skye Causer (10)
Crofton Anne Dale Junior School, Stubbington

A Monster Called Cheese

I've seen a monster that I've called Cheese.
With very long fur and knobbly knees.
I saw her climbing into a hatch.
The hatch of my attic where she left a three-clawed scratch.

The glimpse that I caught.
Was of a gruesome wart.
The only thing she left was a big bag of kale.
And the remnants of her blue and white tail.

I picked up the kale when my mum caught me.
She thought I was munching on what she planned for our tea.
Since our first encounter, I haven't seen Cheese.
Even though I suspect she is stealing our peas!

Mia Hogg (9)
Crofton Anne Dale Junior School, Stubbington

Monster Poetry - Beastly Creations

Who's That?

The hairy, scary monster
Sat in the winter's corner
Not knowing what to do
But glaring at you.
1, 2, 3 moonlit blooms.
He's creeping up and, "Ouch,"
Said a little tiny mouse.
"Roar," called the monster,
"Argh!" squealed the mouse.
Stomping off he blends in,
He's coming for you.
His eyes shining bright
In the moonlight.
Staring at a deer,
His big mouth, ready to pounce,
Slurping his spit,
He's licking his lips.
His sharp white teeth
Are ready to eat.

Pari Mistry (10)
Crofton Anne Dale Junior School, Stubbington

My Life As A Monster

Attention please, attention please,
Don't dare to talk, don't dare to sneeze!
My life is crazy, not peaceful like a daisy.
I cannot shout, I cannot speak,
I really am very weak.
I am good, not bad
But my story is very sad.
All the monsters tell me,
"You have to be like me!"
So you see, I am tied up in the middle,
Whether to be big and scary
Or weak and little.
My zoog (dog) is the only one who does not mask,
But now before I go just know...
Don't mask or pretend.
Be you.

Olivia Ward-Saunders (10)
Crofton Anne Dale Junior School, Stubbington

Auty Alan's Hope

Auty Alan needs hope,
So Alan covers his ears,
Too many voices, he can't cope,
He needs to suppress his fears.
Auty Alan is most honest
And likes to have his own space,
Too many eyes make for unrest,
The importance of time and place.
Auty Alan says it's trapped inside,
It won't come out on cue,
Please be patient with him,
'Cause he really needs you.
Auty Alan's hands are flappy,
He can be very silly,
Smooth textures make him happy
So be kind, don't ask Billy.

Eleanor Try (10)
Crofton Anne Dale Junior School, Stubbington

Squiggles The Monster

Squiggles, most people would say they're unique
Well, this monster is messy and he might be from your work
And one of the things we know is that he leaves messy squiggles.
Squiggles is imaginary, he is a very good actor,
If you want him to be he can be your hairy father.

Friendly Squiggles likes all the people who don't scream
And run away and come to his party.
Squiggles is imaginary, he has a squiggle cake for his birthday,
It can taste of any flavour as long as you have an imagination.

Henry Gelder (10)
Crofton Anne Dale Junior School, Stubbington

Cheesy Toes!

After a long hot day my feet began to smell,
I was scared to go home because my bedroom is hell.
For in my drawer Lizzy Long Tongue waits for me
And she eats cheesy feet, last week she ate three.
She leaps out whilst you sleep with your dreams,
Awaiting with her pointy teeth like a stream.
The tongue wraps around your leg squeezing tighter and tighter
Until your leg suddenly gets much lighter.
Your foot drops off and goes plop on the floor.
Lizzy Long Tongue strikes again once more.

Fraya Pugh (10)
Crofton Anne Dale Junior School, Stubbington

Monsters Under My Bed

I think there's a monster under my bed.
That sleeps really close next to my head.
They come out at night and give me such a fright.
They scratch and they claw
Making me think there's someone at the door.
When I have a peek and look who it is coming in
It's a surprise at what I see,
There's nothing there staring back at me,
Is there a monster under my bed
Or am I thinking that in my head?
How do I find out if this monster exists
Or is it just a myth?

Ella Griffiths (10)
Crofton Anne Dale Junior School, Stubbington

Monster Under My Bed

In the middle of the night I woke up to a fright.
I leapt out of bed just as the monster fled.
I looked out of the window at the bright moon
Then I quickly ran into my parents' room.
My mum said, "It's all in my head,"
But I'm pretty sure a monster was under my bed.
Lurking in the shadows, the monster stood,
You could tell by his face he was up to no good.
His teeth were sharp, there was only one thing I could do,
I went to say hi but he smelt like poo!

Isabella Withers (10)
Crofton Anne Dale Junior School, Stubbington

Coco The Monster

Coco is loco,
He is a monster who hides in lockers.
He is only four and he has a little roar.
He likes carrots but definitely not parrots.
His phobia is ghosts but definitely not goats.
He is dusty and crusty
But definitely not a good berry.
Avacodo is one of his least favourite foods,
Same with tomatoes.
His favourite colour is green
But hates his six hour school shift.
He is from South Korea but never North Korea.
Like I said, Coco is very loco.

Kaleesi Joy (9)
Crofton Anne Dale Junior School, Stubbington

The Hive, The Hive

The Hive, the Hive
Beware, he'll eat you alive.
He may look like a normal boy
But he'll gnaw you like a dog toy!
He can be very charming,
But his temper is rather alarming!
He may serve you coffee part-time,
But it will never make up for his crimes.
It will take a gruesome goth girl to work him out
And put him behind bars so he will never get out.
The Hive, the Hive,
Beware he'll eat your alive.
PS: Unless you're Wednesday.

Isla G (10)
Crofton Anne Dale Junior School, Stubbington

The Creepy Monster

I hide under your bed at night
Just like you don't like.
I scare you.
Creep you, prick you, trick you,
Under the light of the bright white moon.
You meet me in your dreams
Of scary tales,
Of midnight frights all around the fire.
I'm great at scaring,
I'm great at staring right into your soul.
I haunt you all your life right until you die
Then you turn into a ghost like me
And we haunt people just like you used to be.

Elliot Deutekom (9)
Crofton Anne Dale Junior School, Stubbington

I Ain't Afraid

I'm not afraid!
I'm not at all!
Not even when I'm playing ball.
Although I am afraid of the dark
But not my friend, Mark.
Uh, what was that?
Was it a dog or a cat?
No! He is a monster!
It has a really scary posture.
It's coming over to me!
Oh no, no, no, help me, please!
Oh wait, it's giving me a hug
And I think I just saw a bug.
Anyways, he's really sweet,
And I think I'll name him Pete.

Aidan Royal (10)
Crofton Anne Dale Junior School, Stubbington

The Lost Monster

My monster is lost
She got lost in Monster Valley
She needs to find her way home.
She could use her phone to get home
She could call her friend, Jane
To help her on her way.
Lost Monster is not scared anymore.
She feels brave
As she sees the whales on the shore,
She is close to her beachside home.
Jane is waiting with me to see her return.
Lost Monster begins to run.
She can't wait to have a hug from me and Jane.

Lily Hatherley (8)
Crofton Anne Dale Junior School, Stubbington

Monster Poetry - Beastly Creations

The Little Monster Beneath My Bed

I have a little monster
Under my bed.

He's blue and small
And not very tall.

He's covered in fur
And disappears in a blur.

Sometimes I try to catch him,
Tug on his very slim limb,
But he's too mischievous
And I can't catch him...

Sometimes I think about my little monster,
Beneath my bed...

If he'll ever come to meet me,
If he'll ever want to play...

Alexa Wu (10)
Crofton Anne Dale Junior School, Stubbington

My Monster Pal Called Fred

There is a tiny monster that lives beneath my bed.
He has large green spikes that pop up from his head.
We always play together, he now is my best friend.
Sometimes he's annoying, he drives me around the bend.
He eats up all my socks, he eats up all my pants.
I know he doesn't mean it, he does it for the bants.
He's funny, he's clever and his eyes are cherry red.
I would never change him, my monster pal called Fred.

Sophie Amey (9)
Crofton Anne Dale Junior School, Stubbington

Trapped

Like a solitary sloth, she waits
Amid the chaos she's lost
Awaiting a saviour to remove her misery
It steals her soul, her heart, her life
Then hides them far away
Where they can't be found
It compresses her organs
Strangles her insides
And the burden she carries weighs down on her
People try calling for her
Nothing works though as it's already taken control
Slowly life fades away from her.

Imogen Stanning (10)
Crofton Anne Dale Junior School, Stubbington

My Monster, Mochi

Mochi Monster's very cute
Sometimes you will hear him hoot!
Mochi's hoot is very loud,
Mochi Monster's very proud.
Proud to be a furry beast,
Proud to eat slugs for a feast.
His cyclops eye is very big,
He smells much better than a pig.
My Mochi friend is not too scary,
Just a little pink and hairy.
Please don't fear him, have no dread,
He's just a stuffed toy in my bed.

Poppy Hewitt (10)
Crofton Anne Dale Junior School, Stubbington

Monster Monster

Monster, monster, rhyme, rhyme
Now it is time to rhyme in time
I've come here to you from Planet Boo
I've brought my friends to see you too
Fang and Hairy love to play
So just like me we'd love to stay
We like to play and have some fun
With you, your friends and everyone
We can't stay, just an hour or two
So let's all have fun, us and you
Then we'll go back to Planet Boo.

Lydia Bradford (10)
Crofton Anne Dale Junior School, Stubbington

Monstrous Malcom Goes On A Mischievous Mission

Monstrous Malcom is his name.
Being mischievous is his game.
Be good to him and he'll be your friend.
If you're bad to him, it will be the end.
He lives in the Congo, where it's hot,
But he loves the beach and a beach there is not.
He's looking around to see who he can find,
No monsters here, only mankind.
He's on a mission to find the sea,
On the way he pulls a prank on... ME!

Jackson Blease (9)
Crofton Anne Dale Junior School, Stubbington

About Werewolf Life

As the night turned cold
And the trees turned old,
The moon in the sky brought out my werewolf eyes.
I roared into the distance,
While the night glistened.
The moon stared at my soul
But then I found a viral werewolf that I didn't really like.
He spoke to me in a language that I didn't know.
He was looking like he was about to attack me
Then I ran for my life
Trying not to be found.

Finch Grant Ros (8)
Crofton Anne Dale Junior School, Stubbington

Mr Spooks

Mr Spooks went to the park with Mouse,
All the kids turned and stared,
Why were they staring?

His prickly hair was gelled,
His orange spots were neatly combed,
Why were they staring?

His four legs were extra shiny,
His eyes were wide and gleaming,
Why were they staring?

He looked behind him at Mouse,
"A mouse!" the kids screamed,
And they all ran away.

Jonathan Higgins (10)
Crofton Anne Dale Junior School, Stubbington

Me And Larry The Lizard

I met Larry the lizard in an enormous blizzard
He was all alone and very far from home.

I rode him back to Botswana then we ate bananas
Although Larry is very massive he's also very passive.

Larry's very scaly and bumpy, he's also extremely jumpy
It doesn't take much might to give Larry a fright.

Me and Larry are great friends
And that's where the story ends.

Solomon Phillips (9)
Crofton Anne Dale Junior School, Stubbington

Monsters

Some monsters are big, some monsters are hairy.
Who knew that some monsters aren't that scary?
At night on the Earth creatures creep, crawl and lurk,
But some skip and some play and some even twerk.
Some children get scared and hide in their beds,
But don't be afraid, just remember what I've said.
Not all monsters are bad, some want to be nice
So open your mind and maybe think twice.

Adelaide Davies Vaughan (10)
Crofton Anne Dale Junior School, Stubbington

Hairy McScary

This is Hairy McScary
I play with him all day long
But when he is scared
He turns into a bear
This is Hairy McScary.

You might think Hairy McScary is big
You may think Hairy McScary is bad
But actually he's very small so that makes him glad.

This is Hairy McScary
His house is larger than a mouse
Because his money is very funny
So this is Hairy McScary.

Sophie Cogdell (10)
Crofton Anne Dale Junior School, Stubbington

Ember's Poem

His name is Ember, you must remember
His claws are as big as his jaws
When his fangs come down you'll hear a loud bang.

He might be naughty and he's forty
When you see him flying it will be mystifying
When you see his fire there will be a wildfire.

His neck is hairy but he is still furry
His wings are long and super strong
His name is Ember, you must remember.

Henry Crocker (9)
Crofton Anne Dale Junior School, Stubbington

Monster Poetry - Beastly Creations

My Monster

M y monster is Fang and he has a gang
O ne eye is low, one eye is high
N aughty monsters are shapeshifters
S ound it makes is creepy... "Kill him... Ssss!"
T his monster is crazy and it doesn't have friends
E very monster called Fang lives in Hell, on top of a bell
R adishes are what it eats and then it goes for a poo on the loo!

Thomas White (9)
Crofton Anne Dale Junior School, Stubbington

Patch Is About

A monster you can't catch,
His name is Patch.
He's colourful and hairy,
But not very scary.
Two yellow, skinny arms,
Four skinny legs,
His favourite food is eggs.
Three red slimy eyes,
His claws are as sharp as knives.
15 sharp teeth,
Hair scattered with leaves,
He lives in a cave,
It makes it hard to shave.
Watch out,
Patch is about.

Jazzy Hudson (10)
Crofton Anne Dale Junior School, Stubbington

Oz The Monster In Paris

I'm Oz and I'm from Paris
And I'm such a menace.
I'm cute and small
But that's not all.
I live on the Eiffel Tower
And I've got the power.
I am bad on the inside
But just take a look on the outside.
Sometimes I'm very naughty,
But that doesn't stop me.
I travel up and down on the lift,
Just watch me drift.

Amelie Williams (9)
Crofton Anne Dale Junior School, Stubbington

Joey The Kind Monster

Joey is a friendly dragon
A cheerful Japanese dragon
Likes eating a lot of food
Keeps him in a happy mood
Joey can breathe fire too
An easy way to barbecue
Joey has many scales
All the way
Head to tail
Joey is my friendly dragon
We sleep together in my bed
A comfy place to rest my head
On my dragon
My dragon, Joey.

Leo Kington (9)
Crofton Anne Dale Junior School, Stubbington

My Little Creature

Stumbling through the crunchy leaves,
It heads to its home, ever so pleased.
Brushing the dust off its very soft fur,
It sits on its chair completely hurt.
Ever so bright and ever so green,
It looks like light but it's never that clean.
Happily heading to where it likes to play,
It says to itself, "I've had a good day."

Lukas Davies (9)
Crofton Anne Dale Junior School, Stubbington

Fred's Shed

My friend, Fred, is a monster with a red head
Fred lives in my damp shed
We dread when Fred gets up from his bed
As his dreadful feet stink up our bed.

What Fred likes to do the most is to cool his head
That's why Fred's head is red
So we take him on holiday to cool his head in the sea
So we can sleep in our bed.

Eva Register (10)
Crofton Anne Dale Junior School, Stubbington

Big Scary Monsters

Big scary monsters,
The ones that get you at night,
They hide in cupboards and behind doors,
Just to give you a fright.
But if you ever wonder what it's like
You will be hiding in the dark and not light
Because it could be a bit bright.

He's large, scary and hairy
Make sure he's not under your bed...

Henry Graham (9)
Crofton Anne Dale Junior School, Stubbington

Beep-Bop

Beep-Bop the monster loves to do art
He thinks of a picture and knows where to start.
When Beep-Bop's friends come to visit
They play fun games and eat lots of biscuits.
His fluffy hair is soft to touch
But he always brushes it way too much.
Beep-Bop may be small and hard to find
But with his friends he always is kind.

Katie Nicholls (10)
Crofton Anne Dale Junior School, Stubbington

Homewookie

H orrifying beast
O nce a week
M ake sure you show your working out
E ven Mum and Dad hate him
W eekly punishment
O bviously a horrible idea
O nly right answers
K eeping teachers busy
I wish he'd leave me alone
E very kid's worst nightmare.

Woody Rawson (9)
Crofton Anne Dale Junior School, Stubbington

Monsters In The Night

In the darkness,
The night monsters come out to fright.
They hide in the shadows
And wait for us to doze.
But we must not be afraid
For they are only made in our imagination,
A product of our creation,
So let us close our eyes and say our goodbyes
To the monsters in our head
And sleep soundly in bed.

Alfie Ludlow-Fisher (10)
Crofton Anne Dale Junior School, Stubbington

Is That A Monster?

I was going to bed,
I turn off the lights,
I got into bed,
But what was that?

I heard a growl,
I heard shuffling feet,
I heard a snuffle
And I heard a creak.

I got out of bed,
I turned on the lights
And I saw my dog, Monster
So it wasn't scary after all.

Ruby Wallace (9)
Crofton Anne Dale Junior School, Stubbington

All About My Monster

S illy
P owerful
O beys me
R ebel
T ells the truth

L ovely
O ver-excited
V ictorious
E ats fruit
R aps.

His name is Sport Lover
And this is all about what he likes
And what he does.

Isla Knott (9)
Crofton Anne Dale Junior School, Stubbington

This Is Bob

Bob is blue
He has wobbly knees
And likes to eat trees.
Beware of Bob he might give you a fright
With his bright pink spikes
Riding around on his fantastic bike
But you will find Bob is kind
So should you see Bob give him a nod...
So be more like Bob.

Pippa Clarke (9)
Crofton Anne Dale Junior School, Stubbington

The Monster

M y monster
O ften eats
N ormally at midnight
S tomping to the beat
T reasure and gold he wears for underwear
E veryone loves him, my monster bear
R oaring happily to his own beat.

Demi Ward (9)
Crofton Anne Dale Junior School, Stubbington

My Monster, Gogoholiday

My monster, Gogoholiday
He chooses to go to Spain
He eats ice cream
It melts all over him.

Gogoholiday is massive
He is colourful and scary
At night-time when it's time for bed
He glows big and bright.

Elliot Vaughan (9)
Crofton Anne Dale Junior School, Stubbington

Beastly Bob

Beastly Bob is part of a mob,
Beastly Bob has a very scary job.
He's fierce, fast and freaky,
He will steal your food because he's sneaky.
He lives in a deep, dark cave and he likes to do...
THE MONSTER RAVE!

Charlie Warburton (10)
Crofton Anne Dale Junior School, Stubbington

Freddy And His Big Belly

Freddy had a big belly
And he liked eating jelly.
Freddy had wellies
And put berries in his wellies.
Freddy was chased by some bees,
He tried to fly and he fell on his knees,
Then he got stung by the bees.

Joshua Knight (9)
Crofton Anne Dale Junior School, Stubbington

Silent Hymns

B obby loves the rain
"**O** h the calming taps of rain," he said.
B eautiful stars fill up the sky, he thought.
B rave little monster in his boat
Y et he never feels alone.

Ruben Cresswell (9)
Crofton Anne Dale Junior School, Stubbington

Monsters

M ischievous
O bstructive
N ow extinct
S mells like a rotten egg
T erribly mean
E normous grin
R oars as loud as a lion
S lithers like a snake.

Andrew Baillie (9)
Crofton Anne Dale Junior School, Stubbington

Mega Monster

There was a monster called Mega
He was from an island called Alega.

He had an annoying sister called Nelly
Who really liked eating jelly.

He loved playing Uno
With his best friend, Bruno.

Jaspar Ball (10)
Crofton Anne Dale Junior School, Stubbington

Monster Poetry - Beastly Creations

Jerry

J erry is a big, hairy, wobbly blob monster.
E very day Jerry jumps out on people.
R oar! he says to make you jump, but...
R eally he'll share his chocolate with...
Y ou!

Lucas Day (9)
Crofton Anne Dale Junior School, Stubbington

Monchouawa

If it crunches your bones
You're sure to moan.
If it's near you'll fear because it's here.
When you blink it'll stink
And your heart will sink.

Caelan Fielding (9)
Crofton Anne Dale Junior School, Stubbington

Marvellous Monsters

Marvellous monsters either fly, walk or swim
Vipgons swoop through the air
Or slither monsters are friendly
Vipgons come from western Australia
Where they love it, where it's calm
It's a good monster because it will love you
As much as you love it
It has friends just like you
And soon, when it's had long enough with you
It will go to the monster beach
Then come back for another start
With who's taken care of him or her better
Maybe you'll start to drift in the air just like your Vipgon.

Mila Kiddy (9)
Great Bardfield Primary School, Great Bardfield

Hippogriff

H uge and gentle
I ncredibly strong
P ouncing and prancing around
P erfect and elegant
O ver the fields they fly
G liding over mountain tops
R ushing above the clouds
I ridescent feathers shining in the breeze
F lying high over the shimmering water
F orever soaring to new adventures.

Ivy-Lilly Humphreys (7)
Great Bardfield Primary School, Great Bardfield

The Elemental Dragon

T reacherous evil,
H uge attack defeats its prey,
E ating a tyrannosaurus rex,

E lemental power destroying a country,
L ike a relentless evil god,
E ngulfing a city in flames,
M entally indestructible,
E normously feared,
N ever will you escape,
T aller than a T-rex,
A stronomy is studied by him,
L ethan attacks,

D eadly claws,
R un away,
A bsolutely ruthless,
G argantuan strength,
O minously hiding in the shadows,
N ot to be messed with.

James Russett (10)
Holy Trinity CE Primary School, Cheltenham

Dave The Blob

D eviously dancing towards the dusty white fridge
A ddict to high-calorie delicacies
V iciously devouring fatty fast food
E ating everything in sight.

T hrottled arteries blocked with cholesterol.
H appily melting into the cyan sofa
E nding his workout routine after a lack of patience.

B lack top hat on the peak of his head.
L onging for a more muscular body.
O minous green-coloured.
B urgers he engulfs.

Cressida Bird (11)
Holy Trinity CE Primary School, Cheltenham

My Little Demon Sister

M alicious
Y eti-like

L ong sharp teeth
I llusionist
T op of the charts for being cute but evil
T errifying
L ady of the manor
E specially bossy

D emonic
E erie
M anipulative
O minous
N ot so cute after all

S inister
I t's not always adorable
S ecretive
T ormenting
E ager to get what she wants
R epulsive.

Mona El Aambri
Holy Trinity CE Primary School, Cheltenham

The Pumpkin Man

P rowling in the dead of night.
U ndead creatures leave the ground.
M onstrous beings come to life.
P ushing out the ground at night.
K in are frightened by its face.
I n the dark it roams the streets.
N ightmares tremble at its look.

M any fear of its name
A s it brings terror to those who hear its scream.
N ight walker!

Freddie Hinton (11)
Holy Trinity CE Primary School, Cheltenham

Billy Billy Bob

B izarre, big, bulky
I ntelligent honed monster
L ike a human with wings
L ike a yeti with claws
Y eeting its prey

B oiling its prey's blood in fear
I rrational
L ethal attacks
L ike a demon but
Y ou would faint with fear

B igger than a skyscraper
O ut of Hell
B ob is strong.

Teddy Longworth (10)
Holy Trinity CE Primary School, Cheltenham

Pyro-Raptor

P rowling around searching
Y anking its victims
R ipping through any armour
O minous oral feeder
-
R apidly shooting razor lightning
A s quick as a cheetah across the ground
P yro-Raptor
T earing people limb from limb
O ld, wise, you'd better not mess with him
R aiding houses for a meal.

Atticus Harbinson (11)
Holy Trinity CE Primary School, Cheltenham

Anto Gaming

A killer personality
N ever cares about other people apart from himself
T oxic green saliva dripping from its jagged teeth
O minous

G alactic ocean colour
A scaly, armour-plated hide glowing in the moonlight
M enacing
I ntimidating
N ever living in his dreams
G igantic.

Anthony Hawkins (10)
Holy Trinity CE Primary School, Cheltenham

Kermit's Envelope Of Trust

My brother, Kermit, used to come up to me
and I used to tell him to go away.
Then the next day I went up to him
and told him how sorry I was
because I hurt my little brother's soul.
My sharp claws got stronger and stronger
and my blood erupted because of how sorry I was
but it felt like an envelope,
closing his trust on me.

Olivia Upton (11)
Holy Trinity CE Primary School, Cheltenham

Hairy Gerald's Personality

H orribly hairy
A nd
I n the dim light it snoops
R azor-sharp claws
Y eti-like

G rotesque gremlin
E ating everything in its way
R eeking breath
A ppalling to all
L ike a nightmare turning into existence
D evil-like eyes.

Clemence Sandeman (11)
Holy Trinity CE Primary School, Cheltenham

The Intimigator

I ntimidating beast
N ever fails to kill
T errifies its victim
I n the forest it lives
M ysterious and menacing
I ncredibly grotesque
G reen scales
A lligator-like
T hick, toxic breath
O blivion delivery service
R epulsive.

Daniel Leong (11)
Holy Trinity CE Primary School, Cheltenham

Meep Meep...

"Meep meep!"
That was the sound of a blobby!
An intimidating, mysterious creature,
Lurking inside your drawer and cupboards.
Along with every crack and corner.
You can find the gargantuan creature loves to hound abandoned houses.
"Meep meep!"
That was a blobby!

Betty Brazil (11)
Holy Trinity CE Primary School, Cheltenham

Skeieton

S neaky, sly, snickering
K ind to children (so he can eat their toes)
E vil and malicious
I mpossible to like
E ating Halloween candy (especially toffee)
T errorising and wreaking havoc
O minous and boney
N icking things regularly.

Aurelie Whitelow (11)
Holy Trinity CE Primary School, Cheltenham

Monster Poetry - Beastly Creations

There Is Something In My Slippers!!!

M alicious smile to stir up primal fears.
E ating anything to dare to strike up to its lair.
L ethal canines slurping gallons of fresh blood.
L ike a nightmare coming into existence.
O val-like noggin melting with every smirk.
W ide-eyed devil.

Cordelia Griffin (11)
Holy Trinity CE Primary School, Cheltenham

Sweet Doughnut

S weet-tasting
P lastic-eating
A lien doughnut
C ute looking
E merald

D unkin'
O bject
U nleash the
G rated cheese
H at
N o
U nripe
T imebomb.

Richard Killworth (10)
Holy Trinity CE Primary School, Cheltenham

The Secret

He's always been with you.
Through your ups and downs.
You may not have ever seen him...
But he's always there
Lurking, waiting for you under your bed.
Melting under that dusty wreck.
He leaves a residue.
Why don't you see?

Skye Franks-Bayntun (11)
Holy Trinity CE Primary School, Cheltenham

Achmed

    A ngry scowl upon its face.
    C hurning with a frenzied pace.
    H urling insults on your tongue.
    M uttering threats to everyone.
    E ndlessly aggressive and mean.
    D arkness surrounds you like a screen.

Sophie Nayna (11)
Holy Trinity CE Primary School, Cheltenham

Bloppy!

Bloppy!
Small and slimy,
Transforming, jelly-like,
Rolling around feeling nothing,
Cute.

Bloppy!
Purple monster,
Shapeshifting, slimy-like,
Feeling slobbery like jelly,
Happy.

Isaac Jones (9)
Holy Trinity CE Primary School, Cheltenham

How Does Giggles Look?

G iggly, sniggly, chuckly.
I ce Age escapee.
G igantic furry friend.
G reat for hugging.
L ike a furry pillow.
E asily upset.
S inister with his words.

Zoia Kobzarenko (10)
Holy Trinity CE Primary School, Cheltenham

Bob

Brick easily smashed
On the muscle is lush skin
Betrays nobody

Funny
Extremely buff
He is funny, trust me
He loves food, especially meat
Trust me.

Milan Bencsik (10)
Holy Trinity CE Primary School, Cheltenham

Gorge

Gorge...
Big, dangerous, creepy
Bad, dark

Meet Gorge
Big, blue, orange
One eye, black antennae
Smelling bad
Creepy, bad red eye.

Esther Chindudzi (8)
Holy Trinity CE Primary School, Cheltenham

Naughty Cocky

C ocktail of rudeness and evil
O bserving its prey
C atching new beings
K icking out kindness
Y elling for evils.

Ann Sajan (11)
Holy Trinity CE Primary School, Cheltenham

What Vision Is Like

V icious
I ntelligent
S igma
I mmortal likeness
O minous
N ever let him know your next move.

Amit Rajesh (11)
Holy Trinity CE Primary School, Cheltenham

Miss Bo

Meet Bo
Big green creature
One eye
Purple, dark hair
Bounces around with boundless energy
Sad, fluffy.

Milly Pargeter (9)
Holy Trinity CE Primary School, Cheltenham

Block

Meet Block
Round orange blob
Seven legs, blood-tipped claws
Fights around with a heart full of glee
Happy.

Eric Ameri (8)
Holy Trinity CE Primary School, Cheltenham

Fangs

Brown beast.
Face like a flower.
No eyes, relies on sound.
Scary hunter, like skateboarding.
Big claws.

Ewan Somerville (8)
Holy Trinity CE Primary School, Cheltenham

Cat

Meet Cat,
My best friend,
She smells like marshmallows,
She is the best friend in the world,
Good Cat.

Lucy Griffiths (9)
Holy Trinity CE Primary School, Cheltenham

Amogus

A nnoying to all
L ifeless
E ager to die
K illable
S tupid and useless.

Aleks Skrzynski (11)
Holy Trinity CE Primary School, Cheltenham

The World Of Meep Johnson... In A Nutshell

That's Meep
Helpful and cute
Tall as a table leg
Born in a nutshell, flies swiftly -
Good friend.

Laura Shone (9)
Holy Trinity CE Primary School, Cheltenham

Creep

Meet Creep
Green monster, sharp
One eye huge, horn, green face
Mysterious, green, fierce face
Happy.

Rex Musasa (9)
Holy Trinity CE Primary School, Cheltenham

Scarlott

Small friend
Purple, soft and red
Kind, little, beautiful
Playful, friendly, helps in the dark
Cosy.

Amelie Beckett (8)
Holy Trinity CE Primary School, Cheltenham

Shme

Massive
Fierce red, blue too
It can run really fast
It is more scary than you think
It's Shme.

Torin Whitelow (9)
Holy Trinity CE Primary School, Cheltenham

Lurkey The Beast

Lurkey
Big, scary, blue
Eats flesh, lurks, slithers, kills
Fearsome, crazy, mad, ugly
Talons.

Ben Gregory (8)
Holy Trinity CE Primary School, Cheltenham

This Is Cookie

Cookie
Small cute creature
Big eyes, blue antennae
Stomping, bobbing along with joy
Fluffy.

Diana Stavreva (9)
Holy Trinity CE Primary School, Cheltenham

Bounce

Blobby
Small orange ball
Two cute eyes, silky soft
He has come from Venus to Earth
Bouncy.

Lottie Greenwood (9)
Holy Trinity CE Primary School, Cheltenham

Hi I'm Glubo

Glubo
Big dumb monster
Ginormous cool creature
Destroys buildings with lots of joy
Scary.

Ilias El Aambri (8)
Holy Trinity CE Primary School, Cheltenham

Chubby

Chubby
Two eyes, so cute
It smells like marshmallows
A lot of different animals
Chubby.

Amelie Weeden (9)
Holy Trinity CE Primary School, Cheltenham

Shadow Demon

Kenny
Soul-sucking beast
Gets hangry all the time
Shadow demon, mysterious
Eats flesh.

Leo Turley (9)
Holy Trinity CE Primary School, Cheltenham

Fluff Monster

Fluff ball
Small red creature
Dark eyes, big mouth, scary
Born in Area 51
Clumsy.

Henry Pardoe (8)
Holy Trinity CE Primary School, Cheltenham

Small Blue Creature

Muggy
Fluffy creature
One eye, huge ears
Loves to shake his fluffy tail
Wonder.

Henry Hatcher (9)
Holy Trinity CE Primary School, Cheltenham

Death

Meet Death,
Flying demon,
Snuggly but horrid,
It can shapeshift to anything.
Scary.

Ralegh Steel (9)
Holy Trinity CE Primary School, Cheltenham

Young Writers Information

We hope you have enjoyed reading this book – and that you will continue to in the coming years.

If you're the parent or family member of an enthusiastic poet or story writer, do visit our website **www.youngwriters.co.uk/subscribe** and sign up to receive news, competitions, writing challenges and tips, activities and much, much more! There's lots to keep budding writers motivated!

If you would like to order further copies of this book, or any of our other titles, then please give us a call or order via your online account.

Young Writers
Remus House
Coltsfoot Drive
Peterborough
PE2 9BF
(01733) 890066
info@youngwriters.co.uk

Join in the conversation!
Tips, news, giveaways and much more!

 YoungWritersUK    YoungWritersCW    youngwriterscw

Scan me to watch the
Monster Poetry Video